# THE ECHO CHAMBER

Also by Michael Bazzett

Poetry
*The Temple*
*The Interrogation*
*Our Lands Are Not So Different*
*You Must Remember This*

Translation
*The Popol Vuh*

# THE ECHO CHAMBER

poems

## MICHAEL BAZZETT

MILKWEED EDITIONS

Published 2021 by Milkweed Editions
Printed in the United States of America
Cover design by Mary Austin Speaker
Cover art © Alec Soth / Magnum Photos
21 22 23 24 25    5 4 3 2 1
*First Edition*

Milkweed Editions, an independent nonprofit publisher, gratefully acknowledges sustaining support from our Board of Directors; the Alan B. Slifka Foundation and its president, Riva Ariella Ritvo-Slifka; the Amazon Literary Partnership; the Ballard Spahr Foundation; *Copper Nickel*; the McKnight Foundation; the National Endowment for the Arts; the National Poetry Series; the Target Foundation; and other generous contributions from foundations, corporations, and individuals. Also, this activity is made possible by the voters of Minnesota through a Minnesota State Arts Board Operating Support grant, thanks to a legislative appropriation from the arts and cultural heritage fund. For a full listing of Milkweed Editions supporters, please visit milkweed.org.

Library of Congress Cataloging-in-Publication Data

Names: Bazzett, Michael, author.
Title: The echo chamber : poems / Michael Bazzett.
Description: First edition. | Minneapolis, Minnesota : Milkweed Editions, 2021. |
Summary: "A collection of poems that explore the myth of Echo and Narcissus, offering a reboot, a remix, a reimagining-and holding up the broken mirror of myth to late-stage capitalism, social media, and our present-day selves"-- Provided by publisher.
Identifiers: LCCN 2021004731 (print) | LCCN 2021004732 (ebook) | ISBN 9781571315380 (paperback ; acid-free paper) | ISBN 9781571317469 (ebook)

Subjects: LCGFT: Poetry.
Classification: LCC PS3602.A999 E27 2021  (print) | LCC PS3602.A999 (ebook) | DDC 811/.6--dc23
LC record available at https://lccn.loc.gov/2021004731
LC ebook record available at https://lccn.loc.gov/2021004732

Milkweed Editions is committed to ecological stewardship. We strive to align our book production practices with this principle, and to reduce the impact of our operations in the environment. We are a member of the Green Press Initiative, a nonprofit coalition of publishers, manufacturers, and authors working to protect the world's endangered forests and conserve natural resources. *The Echo Chamber* was printed on acid-free 100% postconsumer-waste paper by McNaughton & Gunn.

*for Leslie*

# CONTENTS

• • •

• • •

# THE ECHO CHAMBER

# History

*after Jameson Fitzpatrick*

The vinegar tang of a glass of wine
left out on the counter overnight, the hint
of cumin on your fingertips, dried lavender.
All this is the smell of you in summer,
and now it is history. I woke alone

and slid my legs into the twin flannel
tunnels of my sweats, and it was history.
I walked down to the 7-Eleven
for a Big Gulp in lieu of coffee
and this ill-considered choice

was history. The sweet syrup in the mix
had never seen a cane plantation. It was born
of corn, which is what the ancient Maya
said the first people were made of. And yes
this too was history. *Is* history. Our ability
to take a moment here to quibble over verb tenses
is a consequence swollen fat as a paperback
some thoughtless person left out in the rain

of history. The melodramatic line breaks
in this poem are history. Both the relatively justified

length of line and the use of the word *justified*
to suggest things come out even in the end
are history. And the head-fake back there
in stanza one where you thought this might be
about the end of a relationship but discovered

otherwise is history. As is your inclination to continue
trusting me. Because the fact that I can take
the time to write this all down, considering what
to include and what to leave out, as I tap keys
that were injection-molded out of a blend
of thermoplastics by distant people I will never
have to think of again is one definition of history.
One definition. Not the first. And not the last.

# I Travel Back in Time

I travel back in time to find a woman by a pond,
embroidery hoop in hand, her needle
dipping and rising
like a dolphin

                    as she hand-crafts
a selfie.

             She inclines herself to ponder
her image in the water, then chooses a bit of wool
to catch the light that flecks
her eye.

               "Wow," I say. "Awesome."
She blushes and says, "Prithee good sir, speak
not of what inspires awe

              here beside this humble pond
whilst I dabble with my cloth and cord,

                  imperfect as I am."
"Whatever," I say, "It's all good."

This is how I study history. I *go* there.
      I see the sights and smell the smells
which often entail fresh

             dung, spring
             rain, and copious animal odors.

Needlework done, she will hang it on the chestnut trees
  that line the lane beside her home.
                  I encourage her to do this
as a sort of *status update*,
                      to let folks know
            she's *looking good* and *living her best life*,
phrases I have brought her as mantras from the future
            where we are fully committed to such things.
Over time,
            people will learn to drop rose petals
          in the basket beneath her image
                  to indicate their approval
and she will finally be able to count them up
                  to see how much she's worth.

## The Problem

                    was that the miniature
bears that became so fashionable
were prone to hip dysplasia
    so those who had been
                        unable to resist
owning a grizzly the size of a house
    cat were forced to watch
                        the animals
slowly lose the function of their back legs
    and drag their limbs behind them
    in an uncanny echo
                        of a miniature sea lion.
What made it worse
                    was how good-
natured the little bears turned out to be,
    how accepting
            of their fate, as if they'd known
    their legs would last only a short while,
like the anticipatory grins
    of those waiting in line for the Tilt-a-Whirl
            at the fair. People
used to post photos of the bears
    holding plums between their forepaws,
        tucking into the fruit

like a melon. A man in Seattle
thought it would be funny
to film his bear
wrestling with a salmon
but when the fish's silver jaws
gripped
onto the tiny furred limb and both creatures
flipped into the stream
the video went viral for the wrong reasons
and the look on the man's face
as he dragged the sodden hulk
of what looked like a strangely delicate
woodchuck from the water
told us everything we needed to know.

# Movie Night

I am quite proud of my 35 millimeter projector
      and my prowess in creating novelty films
      in which I am able to reverse
      time for myself and a few select friends,
      so I often set up the projector
      and invite the neighbors to watch.

In the opening scene, the end-stopped
      inhalation of a violent sneeze
      is drawn into the tightly puckered
      sphincter of my face
      then relaxes into an innocent
      slackness that never sees it coming.

This draws a fair amount of laughter
      but the kids really cackle
      when a dark and glossy coil
      rises snakelike from the water
      and leaps into my asshole.

From there it curls through the turnings of my body
      writhing through my inner heat,
      where it turns from shit to food.
      I watch myself ungorge the meat

and stitch it together with knife and fork
to be uncooked, wrapped in clear
plastic and driven backward to the butcher
where his cleaver will trace the seam
that fuses the cask of the ribcage shut.

A lovely night, we all agree, standing in porchlight,
  but the children refuse to go to bed
  until we promise we will take them
  to the place where throat-slit cattle
  draw blood from the floor of the abattoir
  then leap to their trembling hooves
  to spit voltage back into the grid
  before ambling tail-first to the feedlot
  where they melt into ever-slimmer versions
  of themselves, waiting to be drawn
  into the womb to sleep and never wake.

# The Campaign

We found ourselves to be quite fond
   of the ad campaign
      undermining late-stage capitalism:

how the sprightly old woman
     kept bursting into private conversations
at the candlelit restaurant

      and shouting, You can't eat nickels!!
and then doing that little hip-hop dance
    that was surprisingly sexual.

But then, over dinner, after draining
     a second bottle of prosecco as the war
   drifted in from the living room TV

    we started wondering how
      effective the meme had actually been,
  given we'd spent nothing

    but money on loving one another,
and the pills our children took were growing
     more and more costly by the day.

# Hunger

They say you catch more
flies with honey.

Dead bodies
also work. The question

is why you want
flies at all.

Trust me. They will come
soon enough.

I've heard they visit
the eyes first.

# The Monster in Late Middle Age

The MRI revealed a tumor in the shape
of an angel, complete with finely wrought
halo and the curved shoulder of a wing
that seemed to hold a faint, fish-scaled
feather pattern. An intern dismissed the halo
as ancillary tissue but seemed fascinated
by the plumage; he clicked and zoomed
on the scapular ridges, and for a moment
peered at the monitor as if he were alone
in the room. The spokeswoman took
a quick pic and posted an image of the growth,
        #visitedbyanangel and #feelingblessed.

"It almost looks as if an angel is straddling
the liver," the intern murmured, "like
a horse—" then caught himself when he saw
the look on the monster's face. "It feels like
a nail's stuck in my organs," said the monster.
"Like someone planing down a door."
His eyes were huge and brimful. "Sometimes
I wake in the middle of the night and I could
swear some tiny creature's gone to work on me
with pincers. I reach down to check and find
nothing but my own smooth skin." "I'm sorry,"

said the spokeswoman, "I don't suppose it's
any consolation you just gained seventeen

thousand followers." "Not really," said the monster.
"What's the use of a platform if all you have
to put on it is meat." "There was a time
when a pile of rank flesh would have really
struck your fancy," said the spokeswoman
with a sad smile. He nodded, remembering.
She reached out to touch his shoulder,
a simple gesture, gracious and restrained, yet
the intern still felt compelled to look away.

## Costume Shop

Inside the mask hot with my own breath
and the toxic smell of cheap rubber,
I look through eye-holes into the mirror
and see a predictably demented clown.

"This is no good," I say, unpeeling the damp
latex skin to feel the cool air of the shop.
"I was told you would have something more
transformative. Something more…

                                    …real."
The clerk goes quiet
then breaks into the grin of an old friend:
"Okay. Maybe I misunderstood. Maybe
we should go to the back room, yeah?"

The hallway behind the counter smells
of corn chips and the carpet is mossy.
 "I didn't realize you'd already
committed," he says over his shoulder.
"I usually get some advance notice."

I nod, not wanting to derail things,
so I'm not prepared when the door opens

and we step into a well-lit examination room
with a tile floor.
                    "So, there are a lot
of different compounds, a lot of different
skins. This?" he says, using tongs to wetly
lift a membrane from a steel tray.
"This is the lining of a sow's
stomach. *Peritoneum*. Very useful."
And he smiles as if he'd grown it himself.


"So what exactly are you looking for?"
he asks, pulling on a pair of blue rubber
gloves with a snap.


 "Well, I'm hoping to look a lot more
like me. And I was told that you'd have
something professional, something semi-
permanent."
                    He smiles.
                              "Permanent is
a funny word. Because nothing is, you know?"
and he flicks a light switch under the counter
and gestures to the shelves behind him,
lined with glass jars, each one holding
a kind of large, veined leaf, slack and folded
into itself as it floats in a clear solution.

14

After a moment, my eyes catch
on what looks like a millipede clinging to one leaf
and I understand it's not a millipede
but an eyebrow and the lightly veined leaf
is not a leaf.

"You should see your face,"
he says, and I wonder if he means the words
as some kind of joke. But he's no longer
even looking in my direction. He's reaching
for a jar, and there it is,

waiting for me.

## Inside the Trojan Horse

And why a horse?

> We loved our horses,
> the velvet of their noses,
> the knowing
> in their eyes, our broken
> stallions nuzzled us
> and we dreamed
> of drumming an unbroken land
> braided with rivers,
> so long infested with invaders—

And where did the invaders lie?

> In an unworded silence
>
> in the stifling interior
>
> in the belly of the animal—

And why?

Appetite—


And why?

It is always only appetite


And if?

If we had built
our buildings as ruins

it would have saved us
so much time—


And how thin was your hope?

Thinner than the skin
on milk as it cools

Thinner than the lilac-veined lids
of a newborn's eyes—

And how many of them were inside?

Few enough
that they kept
their mouths shut

More than enough
to shut ours

And, of course,
they opened the gates—


And how many of them were outside?

Thousands

They crawled the beach
on a moonless night
like turtles
in their armor

Shreds of wool
were tucked

in the hinges
to deaden
any clanking

The wet sand
ate the sound—


And what did they carry?

                    A ten-year, aching, blue-balled
                    rage—


And what did they do?

                    What cannot be undone


And what did they do?

                    They discovered
                    how high
                    you can fling a baby

They discovered
the sound
it makes

when it lands—


And where did the invaders lie?

Among us

Even as we celebrated, drinking
wine deep into the night,
they were always
there, among us—


And where did the invaders lie?

Deep in the courtyard
of the sacred temple—


And who put them there?

We did—

Who put them there?

We did.

# Menu

Once you've found your upholstered seat
and a slightly elevated vantage point
from which to enjoy the war, perhaps
you'll wish to consider our menu.

The seared tuna with lemons, halved
and roasted on the grill, provides an apt
accompaniment to the sophistication
of modern combat. The ruby flesh nearly

melts on the tongue, the bed of arugula
and shaved cabbage serving as a welcome
bit of structure. Might we also recommend
a lightly oaked chardonnay to accompany

the drones hovering in over the desert?
Its slight muskiness complicates the aridity
of what is essentially insect-delivered weaponry.
Our marinated *pulpo* can be followed

by a salad of fennel, dill, and pine nut
that will lightly cleanse the palate.
When the concussion of distant artillery
thrums up through your espadrilles

nothing really hits home like our molten
chocolate gateau laced with bourbon
raked with AK-47 fire then served
in spattered clumps alongside the still-smoking

cartridge. That saltiness you taste
is simply a touch of your own blood
drawn quietly from your veins last night,
while you dreamt of other things.

## The Wall

It seemed the best way
        was to dig a narrow trench, plant
some bricks,
      some broken glass and cinderblocks,
         cover with a thin layer of soil,
add sun and water,
                     then watch the wall
grow. In the early stages
          something might occasionally
still make its way out
        through the spiny irregular growth.
We once found a mule deer
       strung up by its hind legs
            when it did not quite clear
      the height, a slack weight, its eyes
gone.


         "That's very good," said the man
staring at the length of belly
  with pale hair swirled like fine-grained wood,
"They eat everything.
       They even dig up bulbs.
            Think of our gardens."

We nodded. A few of us jotted
*For the love of our gardens.*

The beauty of the wall
            was that it continued to grow
long after its kinks had sealed shut
        and it had become so high
      it informed the flight
                of songbirds.

It was rooted in the red soil
             like a molar
   and its strange yellowish cast
was pale along the ridges

        and mottled with stripes
of guano from the bats who took up residence
      in its overhangs and hollows
           spiraling out at dusk
              to feast on mosquitos.

Over time the wall
   began to appear on maps,
      showing up as a sort of dull
         blade pushing into the atlas,
beige bits of paper furrowing

                    behind it, like a plow.
                         Now if you read
the legend, pale blue
         no longer means water, nor pale green
plains, everything has been bleached
                   white so words can land
                         uninterrupted on our eyes,
as the wall curves above us,
         and our nights are no longer troubled
         by the indifferent stars.

## What I Did

First, I became a lake so that I could never drown.

Then, I became the wind so as not to lose my breath.

Finally, I became fire so that I would be a tongue

and make luminous the murder of what I most desire.

## The Man on the Screen

The man on the screen
refers to imaginary worlds
with raised eyebrows
and such a patronizing patience
that we begin to suspect
he thinks the world he lives in
is actually real. That this
is not a joke. Have you heard this one?
A man walks into a club
with two penguins and a nun.
It's a black and white film from the '60s.
No. A man walks into a club
held by a policeman.
The cop holds it still
while his fellow officers
encourage the man to walk
into it so many times
it becomes a meme. They assist him
once he cannot stand.
One cop picks up the man's slack hand
and begins to slap his face
and say, Stop it! Stop
slapping your own face!
Put nipple-clamps on the old language

says the man on the screen.
Give it some voltage.
We watch the clip again
and again, clucking
our disapproval, shaking
as we fumble through the cushions
for the remote, a word
that means "far from the centers
of population" or "possibility
that is unlikely to occur."

## Career Day

Any questions? I ask
            after my brief lesson on how to field-
            dress a hare with one
slit from neck to hip.
                  I've draped the body
on a wooden drying rack at the front of the classroom
and it is dripping onto the towels
                        I have laid beneath.


Dark towels, to avoid stains. The children
are quiet.
            Oh, come on, I say, there is no such thing
as a stupid question,
                        just stupid people! Finally
one girl raises her hand.


Can you tell us where the mind ends and the world
begins?                    Ah! A philosopher, I say,


playfully brandishing the freshly-cleaned blade
            before I wipe it once more on my corduroys.


Well, I don't know the answer to your question but
I am going to keep talking

                              because I

am a grown-up

        at the front of a classroom. And you, little girl

—what was your name again?

                              I don't have one,

she says, I was a wild

              hare until just a few minutes ago.

# Florida

Watching baby alligators
and their white needle teeth
go to town on the bloated corpse
of an indeterminate mammal
is not my favorite way to begin
a Tuesday. At least I have coffee.

I'll take a walk on the beach, I said,
not planning on seeing a seething
mass of reptiles swarm the hulk
of what was once a domestic pet
and tug at its remarkably rubbery
flesh then jerk their heads back quick
as if tossing back a shot of low-grade
mezcal, because alligators cannot chew.

Watching them scuttle and work
their teeth in a sideways sawing motion
that might be employed by an inebriated
man going after a cheap cut of meat
is a reminder that successful evolutionary
design does not have to be beautiful.

No, it can also be about gnarled things
peeled like bark from the rutted tree
of ancient hunger then loosed to shred
a body you might have called *good boy*
in a foolish lilting voice as you scratched
behind his ears, snugged him
close, and he shut his eyes in bliss.

## Part of the Animal

Feed me the part of the animal
no one wants, the wiry bone
cage of its back, its knotted feet

picked clean and fried with greens
ripped from a dusty ditch. Serve it
to me in a tin can with powdered

glass sprinkled on top. Let me
die slowly. Let the tiny lacerations
bleed it out of me: the poison

they planted so long ago. Allow
my body to return to its human
shape before they find it. Then

no one will be forced to confront
what we have always been, mostly
wolf, mostly ape, far too clever.

## I Decided to Invent a Poet

I thought if she could
tap my veins to write the things I did not know I know
I might overhear messages
as I dragged my fingers over city maps,
my own blood whispering back to me
how and where it aches

I thought I could instruct her to use just barely enough
words to trace the outline
of what ails us, so we would not be distracted
by its teeth or mottled hide

Who would have guessed she would insist
the animal is blind, a worm
in our gut, incapable of sensing
light as it feeds
on what feeds us
in the tunnels of ourselves

• • •

# Echo & Narcissus, Revisited

The story

                  begins, as it always does
            with his mother, a nymph, the color of sky
snared in reeds and ravished
                by the churning river
        god, ravished being

                          myth-speak

for rape.
          So Narcissus was conceived
from hunger
            roused and taking what it
             could
then moving on. Years later, in the shaded glade

when he caught the glance of that gorgeous
          pool boy and got stuck
                on the Velcro of himself,
        we might be tempted to say
      the son
          had his father's eyes.

But Narcissus was never one to see himself

o

in moving water.

He liked his image
still, the pond

barely trembling.

o


When he was born, his mother asked the sage, Tiresias,
   if the boy would lead
            a happy life,


and Tiresias answered:

            If he knows himself – not.

I cannot tell you
    how long the mother worked
    to tease out
           that *not*, that knot
     of possibilities,
         that pause,

        that dash
heading nowhere—

o


    but gods love their riddles
        and this boy
     would hold that riddle
if a riddle can be held.

o


     Would it have been better
if Tiresias had held
        the mother's hand
           looked deeply and sadly
        into her eyes and said

nothing?

o


The boy grew.

o

Have you seen the pale lance
of the lily
pierce the air?

Have you seen the silken petals
of the iris
fatten in their jackets?

Have you seen the little rivers
of muscle
quiver on a colt?

o


So the boy grew.

And yes, he was

        (as they used to say in olden times)

a stone-cold fox.

o


And yes, his mother loved him.

o

Like the soft meat of the avocado
        holds the shape
of the pit that falls clean
        from its buttery flesh,

she held him as an absence,
        an ache, and his beauty made her
a little crazy, to know a thing so
        perfect had lived a while inside her.

I *made* this, she'd say, laughing
        and hanging from his shoulders,
and he'd shrug her off, gently
        at first, then shucking her clean

with the same violent shiver
        his body would use
to shed a clinging lover.

o


    That shiver became a rather useful gesture.

o

Remember: his father was not in the picture.

And his mother was not inclined
        to speak of him beyond mentioning –
            once – that he was a river.

And what exactly do you want me to
    *do* with that information, said the boy.

o

In the film version,
Tiresias reappears in this moment
for one grainy scene.

He holds the mother close,
and says nothing,

but the subtitles read:

        *Life breaks all of us*
        *because we are temporary,*
        *and because we love.*

o

The boy had a friend

           who wanted to be more. Narcissus

told him no. Took his hand

           from his leg and told him

no.


         And that night,

         walking home,

         the spurned lover

         looked at the stars

         and issued a curse:


"Let his hunger mirror mine, taut

       balls and a throbbing ache that comes


to nothing."


 In the looping meme

             unsteadily filmed with handheld

      phone, the jilted boy hollers

"Narcissus," and we see the young Narcissus

           turn again and again

        toward the camera

      to hear the tinny shout:

     "Go fuck yourself!"

and the camera waltzes away, crackling static
and laughter,
having offered all the encouragement
the boy would ever need.

o

When Narcissus was at the age where his sex
quit being the little
blue-capped noun
it had always been and took on the
stirrings of a verb
he started writing little verses:

*Taut root*
*of the air—*


*unseemly ape*
*wanting*
*to mount—*

And around this time,
Echo, a nymph,


was roaming those woods as well, long-limbed, lithe,
the flickering image of the moon

        goddess, skilled
and stealthy at the hunt, she saw Narcissus
       coasting fluid
          as a stag, muscles seething

beneath his skin, and she grew hot
        and hungered to dip

       herself into that river

boy's mouth.

  o


Juno had cursed the girl
      to be a mirror
      made of words.

They should have been

            the perfect couple,

  o


and when Narcissus saw her shadow
       gliding among the trunks

and shouted, Is anybody here?

Echo resounded:
*Here!*


Why
do you run away from me?

*Why do you run away*
*from me?*


Follow my voice
and let's come together.


*Let's come. Together!*


She sprinted from the woods

and leapt into his stunned
arms that did nothing to receive her.
She embraced his neck,
wrapped herself around him
and he shook and shuddered
loose as if
her limbs were made of snakes.
As he fled, he shrieked,
I'd rather die, than let you have your way
with me.
*Have your way with me!*

she cried,
     and fell, crumpled like a cast-off raincoat,
     wrecked and sweating
with shame. She slipped
           into the silent woods
and hid
     in the bone-littered caves of mountain
wolves and bears, no longer hunting but
  haunting,
    filled with an ache that endured,
and even fattened itself
         by feeding on the wound.


o


She remained perfect
  in her affections,
    turning herself into a vast

chamber of nothing,

       hallowing

    the hollow
    where

*maybe?*

the boy's heart should have been.

o

But the boy kept
running.

The sun was hot,

and the boy kept
                running.

The blue
grove
beckoned.

        There was a pool
        of black water.

                A dark mirror.

He sprawled to drink and cupped his hand to mouth
                                and the water

52

tasted sweet as stone,

        and he lay there panting, and the pond

stilled,

    and their eyes met,
        and—

    *O, hello*

        the rest
      is his story.

# Personal

Chiseled white
  male with deeply
inked Maori tattoos
  and mild fascination
with Wittgenstein
  seeks heavily bearded old
testament god
  for possible revelation-
ship including mutual
  exchange of dictums
etched into stone
  tablets, tickling
low-slung shrubbery
  with hovering flame
and proverbial long
  walks on the beach
where you hoist
  me full-on piggyback
leaving only
  one set of prints—
let me give you
  my golden calves
and be your chosen
  one so we can

bring flowers
   to Nietzsche's funeral—
please, no fannypacks!—
   all calls returned
with resonant silence.

# The Summer Pool

Still as glass and ringed by mossy rocks, the pool
seems different now that we've discovered how
to transport people here from the depths of winter.
They come by the trainload, pale and blinking,
shedding their coats as they step from the cars.
They could be creatures hatched from underground
lairs where light comes through in slits.

See the blue veins on their hands?
See the translucent glow of the children's skin?

Soon the exclamations will begin: how they wish
to bathe in the scent-laden air, how they want
to gulp it down. Before dusk falls and they board
the return train, new lives will be conceived.
The lovers will wander back from the woods,
hands entwined, laughing about losing
their return-ticket stubs. They will dawdle
until the very last moment, climbing aboard
as the trees begin to shudder and then
coast slowly past the windows of the train.

For now we are content to watch these visitors
for a few days every June. We sit in our blinds up here
on the hillside, taking notes from these perches
so effectively camouflaged with the green lace of ferns.

# The Play

Scene one: a man pushes an enormous boulder.

It is quite round, like avalanche boulders in cartoons.
His palms are grey and leathery from the pushing.
His muscles strain and twitch like cables.

A second man enters, stage left, holding a pale blue egg
in his fingers. This is the earth. The man crouches, extending
his arm to place earth in the precarious dark, looking

as if he's trying to roast a marshmallow without getting burned.
For the rest of the evening, the audience contemplates
this tension. The play is a comedy, but the punchline,

as is noted in italics in the program, costs extra.
When the house lights come up, a smattering of envelopes
is delivered to those patrons seated behind a velvet rope.

They open them to find cream-colored cards of thick stock,
perfectly blank. A rustling arises as the patrons turn the cards
in their hands, searching for a message; the sound

resembles wind through dead grass more than laughter.

# Narcissus

It's not easy
performing coitus with a piece of mirrored glass,
but I did it, and I now invite you to visit our wall-eyed
children, lying limp on the beach, like pale fish.
I will resist
the easy double entendre and note that their eyes reflected
absolutely nothing as they grew
milky in the morning light. This is our future,
I announce to the tour group gathered in a knot,
wearing name-tags and sunblock.
The ocean
has begun creeping the alleys, flattening into corners
like a wet cat. It is only a matter of time before
it arrives at our doorstep to nibble the concrete
with its pervasive kiss.

## Things to Think About While Shaving

I killed the younger versions of myself by living
up to this present day. Growing old is a form
of gloating decay where your deepest lines are written

by laughter and gravity. Like Seneca told Nero,
the one person you will never kill is your successor.
Time is one bad mother, said Jesus right before that

first nail encouraged him to rethink some choices.
Or maybe that was me, ropy veins rising on these
hands that hold a blade up to my own soft throat.

# Echo Tried to Save Narcissus

by dumping a load of skinned
rabbits in the pond

figuring the bottom feeders
that rose to mob the flesh

would tear at it with their soft mouths
and thus disturb his perfect

image with their writhing.
But even after all that lusty sucking

had worked the pale ribs
down to a mess of tangled baskets,

Narcissus lingered, whispering
he had finally seen

a flicker of what must be
hunger in his lover's eyes.

# The Trail

Overgrown and gauzed with spider webs, the hike took longer than we remembered, but the path eventually descended to the swept yard. A pine had speared the roof. Cedar shingles fattened with moss covered a dank interior, and behind the squatting blackness of the stove, rusted metal cabinets lined one wall.

The latch clicked easily open. Inside, the package wrapped in cloth and duct-taped snug peeled away from the enamel shelf, and when we slit it open, two dolls emerged, smelling of mud. Their stuffed linen bodies were swollen with damp, but the features on the porcelain heads were perfect and unblemished.

We had expected them to look like us. But the likeness was so uncanny it gave us pause. We just stood there, holding ourselves in our hands, which suddenly seemed too large.

When you joked about checking underneath their clothes to ascertain the extent of the resemblance, it seemed like everything would be okay, that we would be able to put them back and walk away. That we wouldn't still be holding them all these years later, trying to remain quiet so they would not wake.

## The Anger Artist

daubed smoky brushstrokes
across his canvas
with a touch that seemed
both nonchalant and blessed

In another context
he might have been a wayward
uncle with ridiculous hair

When the time came for his opening
the audience gathered outside
the windows of the gallery
beyond the velvet rope
clipped to a brass standard

They shouldered one into the other
eyes wild with hope
until hours beyond the time
the doors were supposed to open

He stood unrecognized among them
fomenting insurrection
until they finally turned and battered him
with a thousand kicks

and a woman drove a pen
into the soft meat of him

He used the blood to write
their most private thoughts
onto the windowpanes, again and again

# Six Mirrors

1. Rude stick figure on a plaster wall

2. Blue glass bottle with smoke curling out

3. A blind man sitting cross-legged on your dresser, making jokes about your looks based solely on the sound of your voice

4. A slab of Carrera marble that you polish with a cotton cloth until a single gray eye emerges, blinks once, then disappears

5. A crisp hundred-dollar bill thumbtacked to the wall

6. Your mother looking down at you, cooing. She is massive. You are held in her arms. The smell of milk. You are beautiful, she insists. So beautiful. Her voice trembles at the fact of it

## At Fifty

My children are beautiful. They grow
away from me like new
shoots from a storm-cleaved tree and I
am dying. It only sounds
like a hackneyed melodrama
because it is. I cry openly when my son slips
onto his bicycle and spins
into the world. We used to ride
together all these mornings.
He pedaled the trail-a-bike, chattering.
My little outboard motor.
Then, his own. He exulted in the balance,
the speed. The days
are far too long, the years
quick as a whisper. My wife
just smiles and shakes her head
at the softness of a man
who has never held a separate heart-
beat in his body. She indulges
no illusions. There's no escaping
the echoing hallway in the temple.
There's a reason it's built
from ossified bone.
Leaving teeth and gold bands,

maybe one incongruous strand
of hair. But this is hardly a rant
about death. It's too in love with life
leaving us, on a bicycle.
Strangely tall now, suddenly
handsome, not once looking back.

• • •

# The Singular Library of Mr. N_____

Every night, he returns home and reads the same book.
He owns only the one volume. The cover is black leather,
soft as a glove, the pages bible-thin and edged in red.
A satin ribbon marks his place.

The thing is, it is always the same book. But what it says
changes. With every reading. Sometimes just a word or two.
Sometimes bigger things.

Like, how the house where the family finds the doll
now has a cellar. Before, it was just a crawl space, mentioned
almost as an afterthought. He doesn't understand how
a house can grow

                                    a cellar. But
there it is, on page 74,
with "a dirt floor that held the smell of roots and damp,
                and dead flies littering its clouded window."

The parents are still rummaging through the pantry
when they discover the doll. They are still shocked to see how
it resembles their son. And it still comes quietly to life while
they sleep, dragging its damaged leg behind as it steals
into the woods. But now the house

                        has a cellar. Weird,

he thinks, letting the book fall closed as he tries to remember
the first time he read it, when there was no family, no house,
no cellar, nothing

     but a boy and a pond in the woods.

# Secrets

Alone in the field,
a man drives a spade into the dark earth and
heaves it open

     so it gasps in soft exhalation.

*What are you looking for?* I ask.

The smell of wild allium rises, green
and sharp. The field is littered
with hulks the size of groundhogs,
as if some weird war has been waged.
Their backs are furred in turf and look
too much like bodies.

*Secrets*, he says, without looking up.

Behind him, in the marsh, a white
heron uproots and floats
across the water, like pale smoke.

*Any secrets in particular?*

The spade shines dull in the last
light. It is dusk. The man turns
one more spadeful of earth.
His shirt hangs heavy
with sweat: *I want to know*

*why a dog will lick the hands*
*of the man who beats him.*

# Echo

Remember when we used to
remember things, she asks.

And for a moment he looks
up from his phone. Yeah
he says. Then, gently,
What made you think of that?

Nothing, she says. It's just—
Having memories was nice.

He nods and smiles absent-
mindedly as he scrolls.

Outside the snow falls
heavily into the lake,
ton after ton of silence
disappearing into itself—

# La Avenida de Santo Narciso

*after Robert Hass*

He camps outside my door,
lonesome, carnivorous.
    His eyes snip into me
with tiny bites. I drop
        coins on his dirty blanket.
He does not blink. Days
        become weeks. He brings me
            smudged photographs
        cadged from the museum,
reproductions too damaged
        to sell. The occasional
            half-bottle of wine,
        stoppered with a bit of rag.
I drink it late at night
            and wake late to a too-high
        sun mapping the floor.
How hungrily he looks at
        the world, at my comings
            and goings. Summer-browned,
        canine, he possesses only
a latent animal innocence.
        I think of bodies on the beach.
            Odysseus caked in salt,

reduced to hinge and limb,
half-drowned, mammalian.
    And what is Odysseus now? A name.
        A Honda minivan.
    And what am I? His heaven.
Me with my briefcase
        living in this body for a while
            before melting back to dirt.
    And so it is we turn into
flowers, and so it is boys turn
        to earth. And even so
            we love the slow dissolve,
        the hush that comes
when the lights go out.

## The Procedure

It is over almost before

                              it begins: the blade drawn quick
across the throat, air
exhaling softly from the trachea as the body

                                slackens into its final posture.
The mouth gapes. The lips

                           pucker into the meditative *O*
of a sunfish held snug as you work to free the hook. Morphine
made the sleep deep and though dark
blood soaks the mattress,

                              there is an air of release if not
relief.

                         Later, when the body awakens,
pale and drained yet saying it feels lighter, the gods
explain that the man inside the body

                            *is* lighter, more than
a gallon empties out, they say with a smile. That's twelve
and a half pounds you won't

                           have to carry around anymore.
And what about this?

                    he asks, gently tracing the slit in his wind-
pipe with one finger. Turtlenecks

                       for a week, and then it

closes on its own. Just don't let anything slip inside until then,
they say with a laugh.


He smiles faintly, takes the pen and clipboard they offer
to sign the release.          So pretty much anything goes now,
right?          Bacon, single-malt, cigarettes?          Heroin?

Meth?

                    Get ready to consume, they say.
You can drink

          a goblet of melted butter if you want.


                              The man signs his name
with a curlicue, hands back the pen.

                    My fingers are *so* white, he says.
Almost translucent, like

                    those weird fish that live in caves.


Honestly, one god says, you couldn't be more white than you are
right now.          Your body has finally been relieved

of duty. All the trouble drained away. The man nods
then

                              smiles and says,
          So, how long until my appetite returns?

# This Line Means Nothing

*for Tadeusz Dabrowski*

This line means nothing

until you read it
and then it's already three lines

back and means something
different than


when you read it first

and now it's
something we're changing


together because
you aren't exactly the same

person you were
when first you read it and I

am not even here

but then again, you might
say, how many poems

about death end
with anything other


than an absent author,
a question mark

# The Epidemic

Where it began is disputed.
The current consensus says probably
the back alley of a quiet neighborhood
where the houses are stacked
like old pottery on the hill above town.
Bougainvillea overhang the balconies there,
dropping petals onto the byzantine
network of narrow paths and stairs below.
I remember pausing on those steps
as my son and I descended to school.
Boys were hunched in the bluish shadows,
worrying a scorpion with a stick. Its pincers
lifted awkwardly, its gold armor stunned
slow by the cold. My son was still
young enough to hold my hand reflexively
but old enough to drop it once
the boys looked up. A distant bell rang.
A look circulated among the knot.
Before the bell finished clanging, they started
down the hill in their matching sweaters,
one stepping back almost as an afterthought
to grind the scorpion beneath the heel
of a sturdy black shoe before jogging off
to rejoin the pack. Only in recollection

did I realize none of the boys had spoken.
And when I later read about the epidemic of
silence spreading among the neighborhoods
above town, I thought of that morning.

# A Stone

wrote a book of poems,

seventy-odd pages
and each one empty.

It was called *happy to wait,*

and its cover was a turtle shell
scoured by weasels,
left abandoned on the beach.

Its sun-bleached husk
was blank as air.
It took years to read,

mostly because the smell
of sunlight and dust
that rose from its pages

was so distracting,
the way it conjured
mountains out of nothing,

the way it made us
drop what we were doing,
stare out the window,

and conjure mountains
out of nothing.

# After Mr. and Mrs. God Died,

I entered their house
and walked through the rooms

that held the silences
of what remained unsaid
throughout their lives

the furniture kept
the impression of their bodies

it stood in the darkness
patient as livestock

and when I stepped outside
to exhale

the silence of rock and pine
insulated under snow
had no words in it

it was empty as a cathedral

I could feel the difference
      between the two silences

and I could hear the trees
      holding their rings inside their bodies

          and I knew I could do
              anything

          except believe—

## The Comedian

The comedian slips the mic from its stand,
gathers the excess cord in a loop, and placidly
stares at the audience.

A few people titter expectantly. He paces,
stops, shifts his weight to one foot,
and the murmur dies away. The comedian's
eyes roam the crowd. He raises an eyebrow.
A woman guffaws. A ripple of laughter.
Time passes.

The audience shift in their chairs, making
papery sounds. A man clears his throat.
"Come *on*," someone shouts. More minutes
pass. A few people shake their heads, chuckling.
Others sit stoic, not chuckling at all.

Whispers simmer through the crowd,
and people begin gesturing to one another,
"Is *this* the joke? Us?" Near the back someone
says a name, Andy Kaufman, as explanation.

After seven minutes, the comedian slips the mic
back into its holster, and whispers,

"You have been a great audience. Ever since
you were born—"

His voice breaks. He is still
as glass. It seems he might shatter. Instead,
he begins to take off his clothes. There are more
clothes underneath. And then more clothes
underneath. Eventually his body begins
to peel away,

           and it becomes clear he's not
a man but a slender woman. And then no longer
a woman but a heron. And not a heron but
a blade. And not a blade but the light

                it catches as it falls,
and soon he is not even that.

# Acknowledgments

I'd like to express my gratitude to the editors of the following magazines, where a number of these poems first appeared:

32 Poems: *The Singular Library of Mr. N*
The American Poetry Review: *The Campaign, Menu, The Monster in Late Middle Age, The Play, & Echo*
Architrave Press: *Personal, This Line Means Nothing*
Beloit Poetry Journal: *The Comedian*
The Cincinnati Review: *The Procedure, The Trail*
Copper Nickel: *Inside the Trojan Horse*
The Freshwater Review: *The Anger Artist*
Image: *Things to Think About While Shaving*
The Literary Review: *Narcissus*
Poetry Northwest: *Echo & Narcissus, Revisited*
Salamander: *Costume Shop*
The Sewanee Review: *History, Secrets*
The Shallow Ends: *What I Did*
Sixth Finch: *Echo Tried to Save Narcissus*
The Southeast Review: *Career Day*
Southern Indiana Review: *Six Mirrors*
The Threepenny Review: *A Stone*
Thrush: *The Epidemic*

Tin House: *The Problem*
Waxwing: *At Fifty, Part of the Animal*
West Branch: *Hunger*

A thousand thanks, too, to all those who were kind to me and these poems; to Charles Martin for his luminous translation of Ovid; to everyone at Milkweed Editions, without whom you'd be holding a handful of air—and my endless gratitude, as always, to my family.

**Michael Bazzett** is the author of *You Must Remember This*, which received the 2014 Lindquist & Vennum Prize for Poetry; *Our Lands Are Not So Different*; and *The Interrogation*. He is also the translator of *The Popul Vuh*, the first English-verse translation of the Mayan creation epic, and the chapbook *The Temple*. His poems have appeared in numerous publications, including *Ploughshares*, *The Sun*, *Massachusetts Review*, *Pleiades*, and *Best New Poets*. A longtime faculty member at The Blake School, Bazzett has received the Bechtel Prize from Teachers & Writers Collaborative and is a 2017 National Endowment for the Arts Fellow. He lives in Minneapolis.

milkweed
editions

Founded as a nonprofit organization in 1980, Milkweed
Editions is an independent publisher. Our mission is to
identify, nurture and publish transformative literature, and
build an engaged community around it.

Milkweed Editions is based in Bdé Óta Othúŋwe
(Minneapolis) within Mní Sota Makhóčhe, the traditional
homeland of the Dakhóta people. Residing here since
time immemorial, Dakhóta people still call Mní Sota
Makhóčhe home, with four federally recognized Dakhóta
nations and many more Dakhóta people residing in what
is now the state of Minnesota. Due to continued legacies
of colonization, genocide, and forced removal, generations
of Dakhóta people remain disenfranchised from their
traditional homeland. Presently, Mní Sota Makhóčhe has
become a refuge and home for many Indigenous nations
and peoples, including seven federally recognized Ojibwe
nations. We humbly encourage our readers to reflect upon
the historical legacies held in the lands they occupy.

milkweed.org

Interior design by Tijqua Daiker and Mary Austin Speaker
Typeset in Adobe Caslon Pro

Adobe Caslon Pro was created by Carol Twombly
for Adobe Systems in 1990. Her design was inspired by
the family of typefaces cut by the celebrated engraver
William Caslon I, whose family foundry served
England with clean, elegant type from the early
Enlightenment through the turn of the
twentieth century.